KIM SCHAEFER'S
SkinnyQuilts

15 Bed Runners, Table Toppers & Wallhangings

C&T PUBLISHING

Text copyright © 2012 by Kim Schaefer

Photography and Artwork copyright © 2012 by C&T Publishing, Inc.

Publisher: Amy Marson

Creative Director: Gailen Runge

Acquisitions Editor: Susanne Woods

Editor: Lynn Koolish

Technical Editor: Helen Frost

Cover Designer: April Mostek

Book Designer: Kerry Graham

Production Coordinator: Jenny Davis

Production Editors: Alice Mace Nakanishi and S. Michele Fry

Illustrator: Wendy Mathson

Photography by Christina Carty-Francis and Diane Pedersen of C&T Publishing, Inc., unless otherwise noted

Published by C&T Publishing, Inc., P.O. Box 1456, Lafayette, CA 94549

Library of Congress Cataloging-in-Publication Data

Schaefer, Kim, 1960-

  Kim Schaefer's skinny quilts : 15 bed runners, table toppers & wallhangings / Kim Schaefer.

    p. cm.

  ISBN 978-1-60705-439-9 (soft cover)

1. Quilting--Patterns. I. Title.

  TT835.S2842 2012

  746.46'041--dc23

                          2011022123

Printed in China

10 9 8 7 6 5 4 3 2 1

Acknowledgments

A big thank-you to the talented team of people at C&T Publishing. You make the whole process hardly seem like work at all.

SPECIAL THANKS TO:

Lynn Koolish, my editor, with whom it is always a pleasure to work;

Helen Frost, my technical editor, you are just the best! Once again thank you for finding and fixing my mistakes; and

Wendy Mathson for the really beautiful illustrations.

Thank you to my longarm quilter extraordinaire, Diane Minkley of Patched Works, Inc., for finishing my quilts so beautifully and for being willing to work around my crazy schedule. I appreciate it.

Special thanks to my family for not only putting up with me but for your continued encouragement and support. To my son Benjamin and daughter Ali—thank you for succinct and enlightened color advice. To my husband, Gary; sons Gary Jr. and Max; and daughters, Danielle and Ali—thank you for your participation in the name-the-quilt game. To my husband, Gary—thanks for all you do for me. Keep it up and I may double your pay.

Kim Schaefer's Skinny Quilts

Contents

Introduction

I love the versatility that skinny quilts offer. A skinny quilt can be used as a purely decorative piece in a difficult-to-decorate long, narrow area of the home, such as a wall or door. Or one can work as a decorative and functional piece when used as a table runner, a throw on the back of a couch, or a bedwarmer. A skinny quilt on the end of the bed in wintertime not only looks great but keeps feet toasty warm.

The projects presented in this book are fast and fun to make and not a huge commitment like a traditional bed-size quilt would be. They add charisma and charm to your home and make great gifts.

This book features a collection of fifteen skinny quilt designs, some pieced and some appliquéd. Whether you are a beginner or an experienced quilter, a piecing enthusiast or an appliqué lover, I'm confident that in the following pages you will find the perfect quilt to add a cozy and cheerful touch to your home—one that you and your family can cherish for years to come.

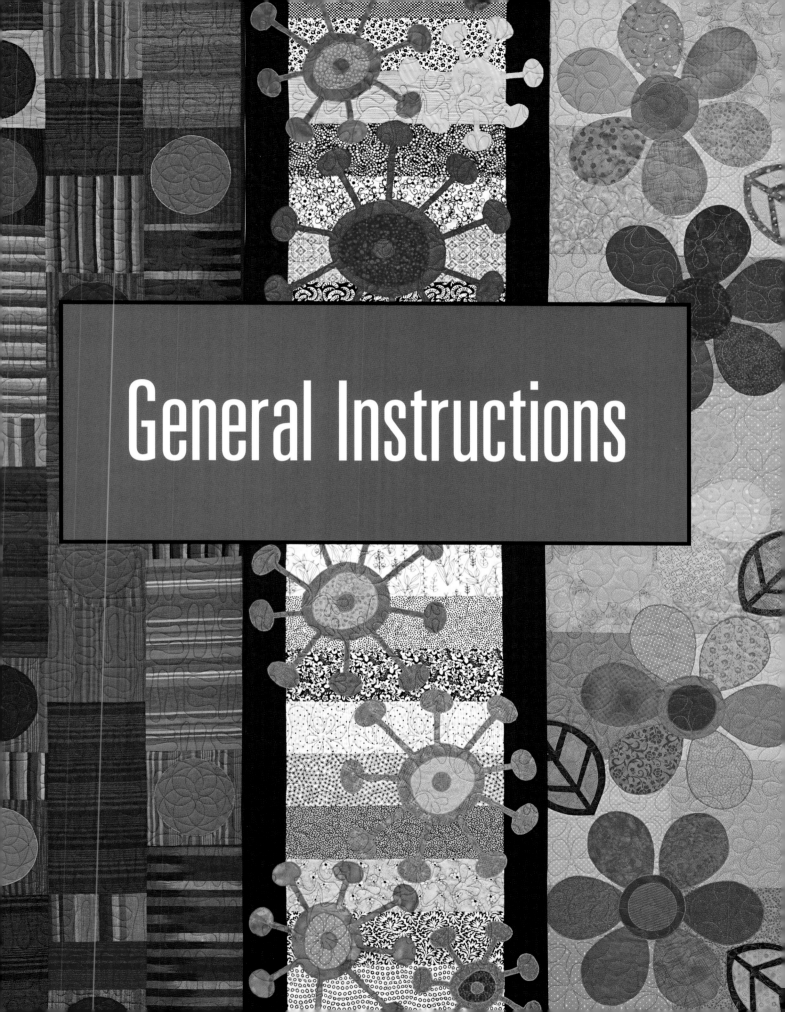

General Instructions

ROTARY CUTTING

I recommend that you cut all the fabrics used in the pieced blocks, borders, and bindings with a rotary cutter, an acrylic ruler, and a cutting mat. Trim the blocks and borders with these tools as well.

PIECING

All piecing measurements include ¼" seam allowances. If you sew an accurate ¼" seam, you will succeed! My biggest and best quiltmaking tip is to learn to sew an accurate ¼" seam.

PRESSING

Press seams to one side, preferably toward the darker fabric. Press flat but avoid sliding the iron over the pieces; that can distort and stretch them. When you join two seamed sections, press the seams in opposite directions so you can nest the seams and reduce bulk.

APPLIQUÉ

All appliqué instructions are for paper-backed fusible web with machine appliqué, and all the patterns have been drawn in reverse. If you prefer a different appliqué method, you will need to trace a mirror image of the pattern and add seam allowances to the appliqué pieces. A lightweight paper-backed fusible web works best for machine appliqué. Choose your favorite fusible web and follow the manufacturer's directions.

1. Trace all parts of the appliqué design on the paper side of the fusible web. Trace each layer of the design separately. Whenever 2 shapes in the design butt together, overlap them by about ⅛" to help prevent a gap from forming between them. When tracing the shapes, extend the underlapped edge ⅛" beyond the drawn edge in the pattern. Write the pattern letter or number on each traced shape.

2. Cut around the appliqué shapes, leaving a ¼" margin around each piece.

3. Iron each fusible web shape to the wrong side of the appropriate fabric, following the manufacturer's instructions for fusing. I don't worry about the grainline when placing the pieces. Cut on the traced lines and peel off the paper backing. A thin layer of fusible web will remain on the wrong side of the fabric. This layer will adhere the appliqué pieces to the backgrounds.

4. Position the pieces on the backgrounds. Press to fuse them in place.

5. Machine stitch around the appliqué pieces using a zigzag, satin, or blanket stitch. Stitch any detail lines indicated on the patterns. My choice is the satin stitch. I generally use matching threads for all the stitching. However, on *Spots and Dots* (page 37) I used black thread throughout. As always, the type of stitching you use and the thread color you select are personal choices.

PUTTING IT ALL TOGETHER

When all the blocks are completed for a project, arrange them on the floor or, if you are lucky enough to have one, a design wall. Rearrange the blocks until you are happy with the overall look. Each project has specific directions as well as diagrams and photos for assembly.

BORDERS

If the quilt borders need to be longer than 40", join cross-wise strips of fabric at a 45° angle as necessary and cut the strips to the desired length. All borders in the book are straight cut; none of them have mitered corners.

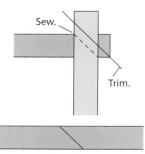

Join borders with 45° angle.

LAYERING THE QUILT

Cut the batting and backing pieces 4" to 5" larger than the quilt top. Place the pressed backing on the bottom, right side down. Place the batting over the backing and then place the quilt top on top, right side up. Make sure all the layers are flat and smooth and the quilt top is centered over the batting and backing. Pin or baste the quilt.

Note: If you are going to have your top quilted by a longarm quilter, contact the quilter for specific batting and backing requirements, as they may differ from the instructions above.

Because I prefer not to piece the backing for my quilts, the fabric amounts allow for the length of the quilt. I use leftover fabric for bindings or add it to my stash.

QUILTING

Quilting is a personal choice; you may prefer hand or machine quilting. My favorite method is to send the quilt top to a longarm quilter. This keeps my number of unfinished tops low and the number of finished quilts high.

COLOR AND FABRIC CHOICES

I have used 100% cotton fabrics in the projects in this book. They are easy to work with and readily available at your local quilt shop.

I have a very relaxed approach to color and fabric choices, and although I have been trained in color theory, I feel most of my choices are intuitive. I use a design wall and usually play with the fabrics before I sew them. I have found that generally the more fabrics I use in a quilt, the more I like it. If you are new to quilting or are feeling unsure of your color choices, that is something you, too, can try.

Thankfully, everyone has different tastes and preferences when it comes to color. In the end, it is your quilt and your choice. What's most important is that it is visually pleasing to you.

MAKING THE QUILT YOUR OWN

If you want to change the size of a quilt, simply add or subtract blocks or change the width of the borders. Many times, eliminating a border will give the quilt a more contemporary look.

YARDAGE AND FABRIC REQUIREMENTS

I have given yardage and fabric requirements for each project, with many calling for a total amount of assorted fabrics that can be used as a base for the quilt. The yardage amounts may vary depending on several factors: the size of the quilt, the number of fabrics used, and the number of pieces you cut from each fabric. Always cut the pieces for the patchwork first, and then cut any appliqué pieces.

The amounts given for binding allow for 2"-wide strips cut on the straight of grain. I usually use the same fabric for backing and binding; it's a good way to use leftover fabric. Cut the binding strips on the grain of the leftover fabric that will yield the longest strips.

Quilted by Diane Minkley of Patched Works, Inc.

Fiesta

FINISHED BLOCKS: A: 12″ × 12″, B: 8″ × 12″, C: 4″ × 8″, D: 4″ × 4″, E: 18″ × 6″, F: 6″ × 6″, G: 12″ × 4″, H: 8″ × 8″, I: 16″ × 4″

FINISHED QUILT: 24½″ × 70½″

I love the modern fabrics in this quilt. Although the fabrics are commercial, they have a hand-dyed look. The combination of brights and earth tones gives this quilt its visual impact.

MATERIALS

3 yards total assorted brights and earth tones for pieced blocks

2¼ yards for backing and binding

28″ × 74″ batting

CUTTING

The pieces for each matching set of squares and rectangles are listed together.

Cut for Block A (Makes 4):

■ 4 squares 2½″ × 2½″ for centers

■ 8 squares 2½″ × 2½″ and 8 rectangles 2½″ × 6½″

■ 8 rectangles 2½″ × 6½″ and 8 rectangles 2½″ × 10½″

■ 8 rectangles 1½″ × 10½″ and 8 rectangles 1½″ × 12½″

Cut for Block B (Makes 1):

- 1 rectangle 2½" × 6½" for center
- 2 rectangles 1½" × 6½" and 2 rectangles 1½" × 4½"
- 2 rectangles 1½" × 8½" and 2 rectangles 1½" × 6½"
- 2 rectangles 1½" × 10½" and 2 rectangles 1½" × 8½"

Cut for Block C (Makes 9):

- 9 rectangles 2½" × 6½" for centers
- 18 rectangles 1½" × 6½" and 18 rectangles 1½" × 4½"

Cut for Block D (Makes 6):

- 6 squares 2½" × 2½" for centers
- 12 rectangles 1½" × 2½" and 12 rectangles 1½" × 4½"

Cut for Block E (Makes 1):

- 1 rectangle 2½" × 14½" for center
- 2 rectangles 1½" × 14½" and 2 rectangles 1½" × 4½"
- 2 rectangles 1½" × 16½" and 2 rectangles 1½" × 6½"

Cut for Block F (Makes 1):

- 1 square 2½" × 2½" for center
- 2 rectangles 1½" × 2½" and 2 rectangles 1½" × 4½"
- 2 rectangles 1½" × 4½" and 2 rectangles 1½" × 6½"

Cut for Block G (Makes 6):

- 6 rectangles 2½" × 10½" for centers
- 12 rectangles 1½" × 10½" and 12 rectangles 1½" × 4½"

Cut for Block H (Makes 2):

- 2 squares 2½" × 2½" for centers
- 4 rectangles 1½" × 2½" and 4 rectangles 1½" × 4½"
- 4 rectangles 1½" × 4½" and 4 rectangles 1½" × 6½"
- 4 rectangles 1½" × 6½" and 4 rectangles 1½" × 8½"

Cut for Block I (Makes 1):

- 1 rectangle 2½" × 14½" for center
- 2 rectangles 1½" × 14½" and 2 rectangles 1½" × 4½"

PIECING

Piece the blocks as shown. Press as each piece is added.

Block A

Step 1

Step 2

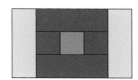

Step 3

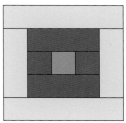

Step 4

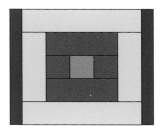

Step 5

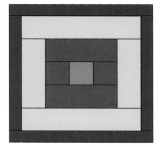

Step 6—Make 4.

Block B

Step 1

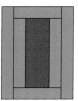

Step 2

Step 3

Step 4

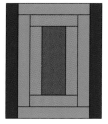

Step 5

Step 6—Make 1.

Block C

Step 1

Step 2—Make 9.

Block D

Step 1

Step 2—Make 6.

Block E

Step 1

Step 2

Step 3

Step 4—Make 1.

Block F

Step 1

Step 2

Step 3

Step 4—Make 1.

Block G

Step 1

Step 2—Make 6.

Block H

Step 1

Step 2

Step 3

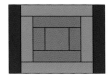

Step 4

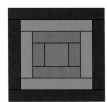

Step 5

Step 6—Make 2.

Block I

Step 1

Step 2—Make 1.

PUTTING IT ALL TOGETHER

1. Referring to the diagram, arrange and sew the blocks in sections. Press.

2. Sew the sections together to form the top. Press.

FINISHING

1. Layer the quilt top with batting and backing. Baste or pin.

2. Quilt as desired and bind.

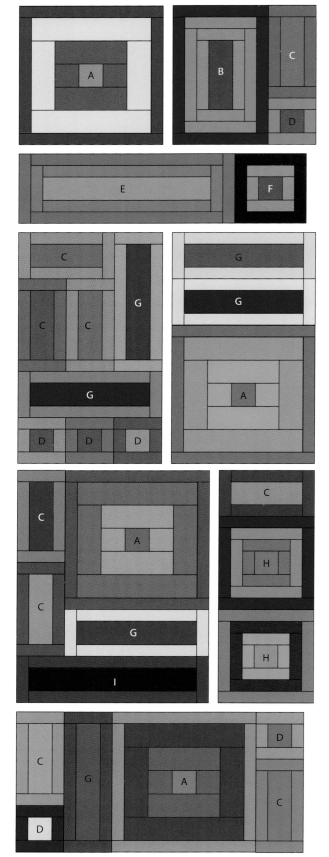

Putting it all together

Happy Jacks

FINISHED QUILT: 22½″ × 90½″

Brightly colored appliquéd jacks are scattered over a pieced black-and-white background, creating visual contrast for this contemporary folk art quilt.

MATERIALS

1½ yards total assorted black-and-white prints for pieced background

½ yard each of red, purple, orange, light green, pink, and blue for appliquéd jacks

¼ yard each of red, purple, orange, light green, pink, and blue for appliquéd jack centers

⅓ yard each of teal, medium green, and yellow for appliquéd jacks

⅛ yard each of teal, medium green, and yellow for appliquéd jack centers

3¼ yards black for border, backing, and binding

4 yards paper-backed fusible web

26″ × 94″ batting

CUTTING

Cut from assorted black-and-white prints:

- 21 rectangles 4½″ × 16½″ for pieced background

Cut from black:

- 2 strips 3½″ × 84½″ for 2 side borders

- 2 strips 3½″ × 22½″ for end borders

Quilted by Diane Minkley of Patched Works, Inc.

PUTTING IT ALL TOGETHER

Piecing

Referring to the diagram at right, arrange and sew the rectangles together for the pieced background. Press.

Border

1. Sew the 2 side borders to the quilt top. Press toward the borders.

2. Sew the 2 end borders to the quilt top. Press toward the borders.

Appliqué

Refer to Appliqué (page 6). Appliqué patterns are on pullout page P2.

1. Cut 1 each of pattern pieces 1–3 for A. Cut 2 each of pattern pieces 4–6 for B. Cut 3 each of pattern pieces 7–12 for C and D. The dotted lines on the outer pieces indicate the leg placement.

2. Create your own outer ring for each jack pattern using template patterns 13–16. Small variations in the size of each leg will give a more folk look. Cut 10 of pattern piece 13 for A, 9 of pattern piece 14 for each B, 8 of pattern piece 15 for each C, and 7 of pattern piece 16 for each D.

3. Arrange the pieces to make 1 of A, 2 of B, and 3 each of C and D.

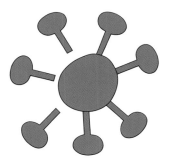

Note: Each jack also can be made as a single piece. Trace the center and the legs on paper-backed fusible web, adding the legs at the dotted lines.

4. Referring to the diagram (below), appliqué the pieces to the quilt top.

FINISHING

1. Layer the quilt top with batting and backing. Baste or pin.

2. Quilt as desired and bind.

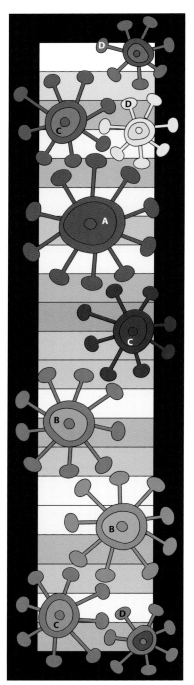

Putting it all together

Village Square

FINISHED BLOCK: 6″ × 6″

FINISHED QUILT: 22½″ × 58½″

I love the rich, vibrant color found in today's batiks. A simple pieced border surrounds the quilt center, which is created by alternating two simple pieced blocks.

MATERIALS

1⅜ yards total assorted medium green and blue batiks for pieced blocks and pieced border

½ yard total assorted dark green and blue batiks for pieced blocks

1¾ yards for backing and binding

26″ × 62″ batting

CUTTING

Cut from assorted medium green and blue batiks:

- 202 squares 2½″ × 2½″ for pieced blocks and pieced border

- 13 squares 4½″ × 4½″ for pieced blocks

Cut from assorted dark green and blue batiks:

- 26 rectangles 1½″ × 4½″ for pieced blocks

- 26 rectangles 1½″ × 6½″ for pieced blocks

Quilted by Diane Minkley of Patched Works, Inc.

PIECING

1. Piece Block A as shown. Press. Make 14 blocks.

Piece Block A.

Make 14.

2. Piece Block B as shown. Press. Make 13 blocks.

Piece Block B.

Make 13.

PUTTING IT ALL TOGETHER

Quilt Center

1. Referring to the diagram at right, arrange and sew the blocks in 3 rows of 9 blocks each. Press.

2. Sew the rows together to form the quilt top. Press.

Pieced Border

1. Arrange and sew 2 rows of 27 squares each for the 2 side borders. Press.

2. Sew the 2 side borders to the quilt top. Press toward the borders.

3. Arrange and sew 2 rows of 11 squares each for the end borders. Press.

4. Sew the end borders to the quilt top. Press toward the borders.

FINISHING

1. Layer the quilt top with batting and backing. Baste or pin.

2. Quilt as desired and bind.

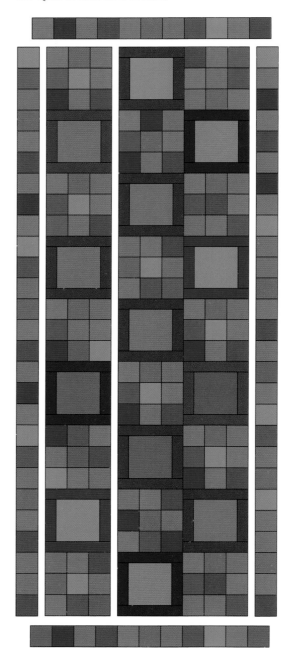

Putting it all together

Leaves

FINISHED BLOCK: 16" × 16"
FINISHED QUILT: 20½" × 88½"

Big and bold appliquéd leaves in bright colors cover this quilt, giving it a fresh, contemporary look. Perfect for the fall season.

MATERIALS

1⅜ yards black for appliqué block backgrounds and lattice

½ yard brown for blocks

½ yard or fat quarter each of bright orange, gold, green, medium orange, and bright yellow for leaf outline

⅓ yard total assorted bright oranges for leaves and pieced border

⅓ yard total assorted golds for leaves and pieced border

⅓ yard total assorted greens for leaves and pieced border

⅓ yard total assorted medium oranges for leaves and pieced border

⅓ yard total assorted bright yellows for leaves and pieced border

5 yards paper-backed fusible web

2⅝ yards for backing and binding

24" × 92" batting

CUTTING

Cut from black:

- 5 squares 14½" × 14½" for appliqué block backgrounds
- 4 strips 1½" × 16½" for lattice

Cut from brown:

- 10 strips 1½" × 14½" for block side borders
- 10 strips 1½" × 16½" for block top and bottom borders

Cut from assorted bright oranges, golds, greens, medium oranges, and bright yellows:

- 104 squares 2½" × 2½" for pieced border

Quilted by Diane Minkley of Patched Works, Inc.

PUTTING IT ALL TOGETHER

Quilt Center

1. Sew the block side borders to the backgrounds. Press toward the borders.

2. Sew the block top and bottom borders to the backgrounds. Press toward the borders.

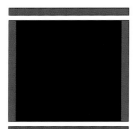

Piece blocks—Make 5.

3. Sew the 4 lattice strips between the pieced blocks. Press.

Pieced Border

1. Arrange and sew 2 rows of 42 squares each for the 2 side borders. Press.

2. Sew the 2 side borders to the quilt top. Press toward the borders.

3. Arrange and sew 2 rows of 10 squares each for the end borders. Press.

4. Sew the end borders to the quilt top. Press toward the borders.

Appliqué

Refer to Appliqué (page 6). Appliqué patterns are on pullout page P2.

1. Cut 5 each of pattern pieces 1–13.

2. Referring to the diagram at right, appliqué the pieces to the quilt top.

FINISHING

1. Layer the quilt top with batting and backing. Baste or pin.

2. Quilt as desired and bind.

Putting it all together

Flip Flop

FINISHED BLOCK: 5″ × 8″
FINISHED QUILT: 17½″ × 66½″

One simple block makes up the center of this quilt. A pieced border frames the quilt center. I used a combination of pinks and browns for this quilt; however, I think it would look great using solids or bright fabrics as well.

MATERIALS

1¼ yards total assorted pinks for pieced blocks and pieced border

1¼ yards total assorted browns for pieced blocks and pieced border

2 yards for backing and binding

21″ × 70″ batting

CUTTING

Cut from assorted pinks:

- 120 rectangles 1½″ × 3½″ for pieced blocks
- 24 rectangles 1½″ × 5½″ for pieced blocks
- 3 rectangles 1½″ × 5½″ for pieced border
- 16 rectangles 1½″ × 4½″ for pieced border
- 2 squares 1½″ × 1½″ for pieced border

Cut from assorted browns:

- 120 rectangles 1½″ × 3½″ for pieced blocks
- 24 rectangles 1½″ × 5½″ for pieced blocks
- 3 rectangles 1½″ × 5½″ for pieced border
- 16 rectangles 1½″ × 4½″ for pieced border
- 2 squares 1½″ × 1½″ for pieced border

Quilted by Diane Minkley of Patched Works, Inc.

PIECING

Piece the blocks. Press.
Make 24 blocks.

Step 1

Step 2

Step 3

Step 4

Step 5—Make 24.

PUTTING IT ALL TOGETHER

Quilt Center

1. Arrange and sew the blocks in 3 rows of 8 blocks each. Press.

2. Sew the rows together to form the quilt center. Press.

Pieced Border

1. Referring to the diagram (page 21), sew together 8 pink rectangles 1½" × 4½" and 8 brown rectangles 1½" × 4½" for each of the 2 side borders. Press.

2. Sew the 2 side borders to the quilt top. Press toward the borders.

3. Sew together 2 pink rectangles 1½" × 4½", 1 brown rectangle 1½" × 4½", and 2 brown 1½" × 1½" squares for 1 end border. Press.

Sew 1 end border.

4. Sew the end border to the appropriate side of the quilt top. Press toward the border.

5. Sew together 2 brown rectangles 1½" × 4½", 1 pink rectangle 1½" × 4½", and 2 pink 1½" × 1½" squares for the remaining end border. Press.

Sew remaining end border.

6. Sew the end border to the opposite end of the quilt top. Press toward the border.

FINISHING

1. Layer the quilt top with backing and binding. Baste or pin.

2. Quilt as desired and bind.

Putting it all together

Quilted by Diane Minkley of Patched Works, Inc.

Lollipop Garden

FINISHED BORDER BLOCK: 3″ × 5″
FINISHED QUILT: 22½″ × 86½″

These folk art flowers remind me of lollipops with their "stick" stems. A simple pieced border frames this quilt.

MATERIALS

1⅜ yards total assorted light greens for pieced appliqué background

1½ yards total assorted purples for flowers and pieced border

1 yard total assorted dark greens for pieced border and flower stems

3 yards paper-backed fusible web

2⅝ yards backing and binding

26″ × 90″ batting

CUTTING

Cut from assorted light greens:

- 16 rectangles 8½″ × 10½″ for appliqué background

Cut from assorted purples:

- 40 rectangles 1½″ × 3½″ for pieced border

Cut from assorted dark greens:

- 160 rectangles 1½″ × 3½″ for pieced border

- 2 rectangles 2½″ × 3½″ for pieced border

PIECING

1. Referring to the diagram at right, arrange and sew 8 rows of 2 blocks each for the background. Press.

2. Sew the rows together to form the background. Press.

3. Piece the border blocks as shown. Press. Make 40 blocks.

Piece border blocks.   Make 40.

APPLIQUÉ

Refer to Appliqué (page 6). Appliqué patterns are on pullout page P1.

1. Cut 7 each of pattern pieces 1 and 2. Cut 13 per color of 7 colors for 91 of pattern piece 3. Cut 8 of pattern piece 4. Cut 1 each of pattern pieces 5–16.

2. Referring to the diagram (right), arrange and fuse the flower stems to the background. A portion of the stem will be covered by the flower on several of the flowers.

PUTTING IT ALL TOGETHER

1. Referring to the diagram (right), arrange and sew 2 rows of 16 border blocks each for the 2 side borders. Press.

2. Sew the 2 side borders to the quilt top. Press toward the borders.

3. Piece the 2 end borders as shown. Press.

Piece end borders.

4. Sew the end borders to the quilt top. Press toward the borders.

5. Referring to the diagram (right), appliqué the pieces to the quilt top.

FINISHING

1. Layer the quilt with batting and backing. Baste or pin.

2. Quilt as desired and bind.

Putting it all together

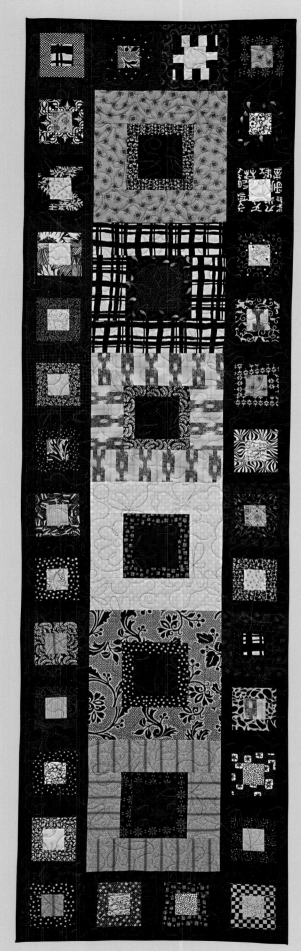

Shades of Gray

FINISHED BLOCKS: 12″ × 12″, 6″ × 6″

FINISHED QUILT: 24½″ × 84½″

A classic combination of black and black-and-tan fabrics is used in this pieced project with timeless appeal.

MATERIALS

1¼ yards total assorted dark blacks

1 yard total assorted medium black-and-tan prints

1 yard total assorted light black-and-tan prints

2½ yards backing and binding

28″ × 88″ batting

CUTTING

Cut from assorted dark blacks:

- 6 squares 4½″ × 4½″ for pieced blocks

- 64 rectangles 1½″ × 4½″ for pieced border blocks

- 64 rectangles 1½″ × 6½″ for pieced border blocks

Cut from assorted medium black-and-tan prints:

- 12 rectangles 1½″ × 4½″ for pieced blocks

- 12 rectangles 1½″ × 6½″ for pieced blocks

- 64 rectangles 1½″ × 2½″ for pieced border blocks

- 64 rectangles 1½″ × 4½″ for pieced border blocks

Cut from light black-and-tan prints:

- 12 rectangles 3½″ × 6½″ for pieced blocks

- 12 rectangles 3½″ × 12½″ for pieced blocks

- 32 squares 2½″ × 2½″ for pieced border blocks

PIECING

1. Piece the blocks as shown. Press. Make 6 blocks.

Step 1

Step 2

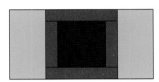

Step 3

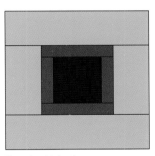

Step 4—Make 6.

2. Piece the border blocks as shown. Press. Make 32 blocks.

Step 1

Step 2

Step 3

Step 4—Make 32.

PUTTING IT ALL TOGETHER

Quilt Center

Arrange and sew 6 blocks to form the center of the quilt. Press.

Pieced Border

1. Arrange and sew 2 rows of 12 border blocks each to make the 2 side borders. Press.

2. Sew the 2 side borders to the quilt top. Press toward the borders.

3. Arrange and sew 2 rows of 4 border blocks each to make the 2 end borders. Press.

4. Sew the 2 end borders to the quilt top. Press toward the borders.

FINISHING

1. Layer the quilt top with batting and backing. Baste or pin.

2. Quilt as desired and bind.

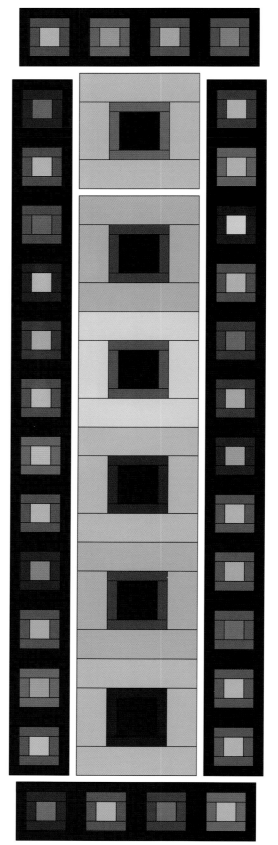

Putting it all together

Flower Pops

FINISHED BORDER BLOCK: 5″ × 5″
FINISHED QUILT: 30½″ × 90½″

The batiks in the background make an interesting contrast with the suede-look textured solid appliqué and pieced borders.

MATERIALS

2 yards total assorted lights for background

2½ yards green for vine and pieced border

1¼ yards total assorted greens for leaves and pieced border

1¼ yards total assorted reds for flowers and pieced border

8″ × 10″ piece of template material

3 yards paper-backed fusible web

2¾ yards for backing and binding

34″ × 94″ batting

CUTTING

Cut from assorted lights:

■ 16 squares 10½″ × 10½″ for appliqué background

Cut from assorted greens:

■ 88 rectangles 2½″ × 3½″ for pieced border

■ 88 rectangles 1½″ × 5½″ for pieced border

Cut from assorted reds:

■ 44 rectangles 1½″ × 3½″ for pieced borders

Cut from paper-backed fusible web:

■ 1 piece 80″ × width of web for appliqué vine

Quilted by Diane Minkley of Patched Works, Inc.

PIECING

1. Referring to the diagram at right, arrange and sew the squares in 2 rows of 8 squares each. Press.

2. Sew the rows together to form the appliqué background. Press.

3. Piece the border blocks as shown. Press. Make 44 blocks.

Step 1

Step 2—Make 44.

APPLIQUÉ

Refer to Appliqué (page 6). Appliqué patterns are on pullout page P1.

1. Trace pattern piece 1 (vine) onto template material. Measure and mark 10″ repeats on the 80″ piece of paper-backed fusible web. Fold the web in half lengthwise and make a light crease. Center and trace the vine template on the fusible web, reversing it for each repeat.

2. Cut 1 of pattern piece 1. Cut 8 of pattern piece 2. Cut 7 each of pattern pieces 3, 4, and 5.

3. Referring to the diagram (right), appliqué the pieces to the quilt top.

PUTTING IT ALL TOGETHER

1. Arrange and sew 2 rows of 16 blocks each for the 2 side borders. Press.

2. Sew the 2 side borders to the quilt top. Press toward the borders.

3. Arrange and sew 2 rows of 6 blocks each for the end borders. Press.

4. Sew the 2 end borders to the quilt top. Press toward the borders.

FINISHING

1. Layer the quilt with batting and backing. Baste or pin.

2. Quilt as desired and bind.

Putting it all together

The Big Easy

FINISHED BLOCKS: 8″ × 8″, 2″ × 2″
FINISHED QUILT: 24½″ × 64½″

Perfect for showing off your favorite fabrics—let the fabric do the work in this simple quilt. Large blocks make up the center of the quilt, and the easy pieced border, made with striped fabrics, frames the quilt center.

MATERIALS

1¼ yards total assorted bright prints for quilt center

1 yard total assorted stripes for pieced border

2 yards for backing and binding

28″ × 68″ batting

CUTTING

Cut from assorted bright prints:

■ 14 squares 8½″ × 8½″ for pieced center

Cut from assorted stripes:

■ 160 squares 2½″ × 2½″ for pieced border

Quilted by Diane Minkley of Patched Works, Inc.

PUTTING IT ALL TOGETHER

Quilt Center

1. Arrange and sew 7 rows of 2 squares 8½″ × 8½″ each. Press.

2. Sew the rows together to form the quilt top. Press.

Pieced Border

1. Referring to the diagram, arrange and sew together 2 rows of 28 squares for each of the 2 side borders. Press.

2. Sew the 2 side borders to the quilt top. Press toward the borders.

3. Arrange and sew together 2 rows of 12 squares for each of the end borders. Press.

4. Sew the end borders to the quilt top. Press toward the borders.

FINISHING

1. Layer the quilt top with batting and backing. Baste or pin.

2. Quilt as desired and bind.

Putting it all together

Feeling Groovy

FINISHED BORDER BLOCK: 4″ × 4″

FINISHED QUILT: 28½″ × 88½″

Big blooms reminiscent of the 1960s
cover this brightly colored quilt.

MATERIALS

1¾ yards total assorted light teals for pieced background

⅜ yard total assorted dark oranges for flowers and
appliqué border

⅜ yard total assorted bright oranges for flowers and
appliqué border

⅜ yard total assorted reds for flowers and appliqué border

⅜ yard total assorted pinks for flowers and appliqué
border

⅜ yard total assorted yellows for flowers and
appliqué border

¼ yard total assorted greens for leaves

1 yard total assorted dark teals for pieced border

4 yards paper-backed fusible web

2⅝ yards for backing and binding

32″ × 92″ batting

CUTTING

Cut from light teal:

■ 16 squares 10½″ × 10½″ for pieced background

Cut from dark teal:

■ 54 squares 4½″ × 4½″ for pieced border

Quilted by Diane Minkley of Patched Works, Inc.

PUTTING IT ALL TOGETHER

Piecing

1. Arrange and sew the background squares in 8 rows of 2 squares each. Press.

2. Sew the rows together to form the quilt center. Press.

Pieced Border

1. Arrange and sew 2 rows of 20 squares each for the 2 side borders. Press.

2. Sew the 2 side borders to the quilt top. Press toward the borders.

3. Arrange and sew 2 rows of 7 squares each for the 2 end borders. Press.

4. Sew the 2 end borders to the quilt top. Press toward the borders.

Appliqué

Refer to Appliqué (page 6). Appliqué patterns are on pages 33 and 34.

1. Cut 5 each of pattern pieces 1 and 2. Cut 30 of pattern piece 3. Cut 5 each of pattern pieces 4–10. Cut 44 of pattern piece 11.

2. Referring to the diagram, appliqué the pieces to the quilt top.

FINISHING

1. Layer the quilt top with batting and backing. Baste or pin.

2. Quilt as desired and bind.

Putting it all together

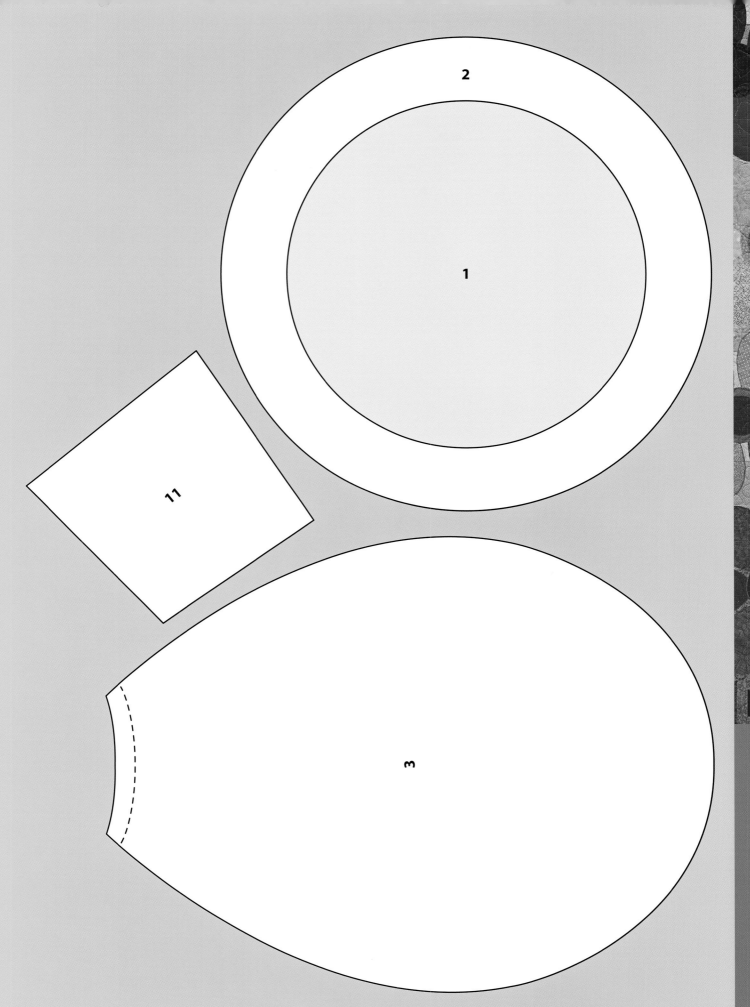

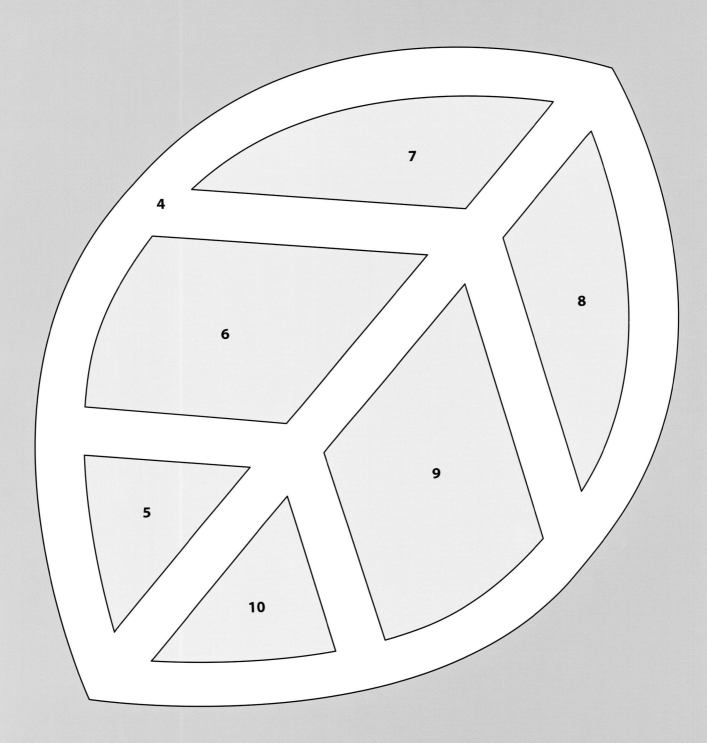

Cotton Candy

FINISHED BLOCK: 4″ × 6″

FINISHED QUILT: 12½″ × 66½″

Soft pastel hand-dyed fabrics are used to create this easy-to-piece quilt with a modern look.

MATERIALS

1¼ yards total assorted pastels for pieced blocks

¼ yard gray for pieced blocks

2 yards for backing and binding

16″ × 70″ batting

CUTTING

Cut from assorted pastels:

- 33 squares 1½″ × 1½″ for pieced blocks
- 33 rectangles 1½″ × 2½″ for pieced blocks
- 33 rectangles 2½″ × 4½″ for pieced blocks
- 33 rectangles 3½″ × 4½″ for pieced blocks

Cut from gray:

- 33 squares 1½″ × 1½″ for pieced blocks

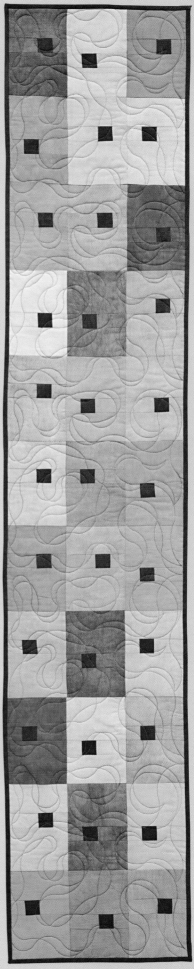

Quilted by Diane Minkley of Patched Works, Inc.

PIECING

Block A

Piece Block A as shown. Press. Make 22 blocks.

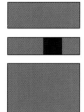

Piece Block A.

Make 22.

Block B

Piece Block B as shown. Press. Make 11 blocks.

Piece Block B.

Make 11.

PUTTING IT ALL TOGETHER

1. Arrange and sew the blocks in 11 rows of 3 blocks each. Press.

2. Sew the rows together to form the quilt top. Press.

FINISHING

1. Layer the quilt top with batting and backing. Baste or pin.

2. Quilt as desired and bind.

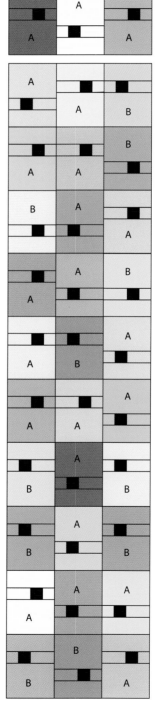

Putting it all together

Spots and Dots

FINISHED QUILT: 22½″ × 76½″

Simple circles are tossed on a plain black background for this modern quilt.

MATERIALS

1¼ yards total assorted brights for appliquéd circles

2¼ yards black for appliqué background

2 yards paper-backed fusible web

2¼ yards for backing and binding

25″ × 79″ batting

CUTTING

Cut from black:

- 1 rectangle 22½″ × 76½″ for appliqué background

Quilted by Diane Minkley of Patched Works, Inc.

APPLIQUÉ

Refer to Appliqué (page 6). Appliqué patterns are on pullout page P1.

1. Cut 3 of pattern piece 1 (3″ circle). Cut 4 of pattern piece 2 (4″ circle). Cut 1 of pattern piece 3 (5″ circle). Cut 2 each of pattern pieces 4, 5, and 6 (6″, 7″, and 8″ circles). Cut 4 of pattern piece 7 (9″ circle). Cut 2 of pattern piece 8 (half of 7″ circle). Cut 1 of pattern piece 9 (half of 8″ circle).

2. Referring to the diagram, appliqué the pieces to the background.

FINISHING

1. Layer the quilt top with batting and backing. Baste or pin.

2. Quilt as desired and bind.

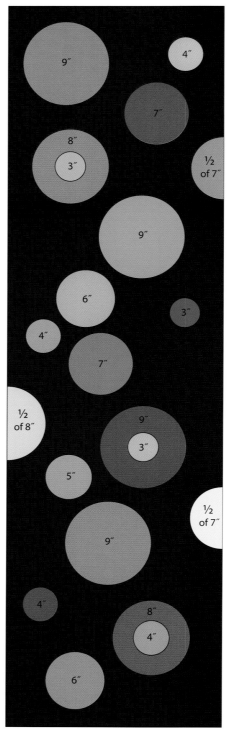

Putting it all together

Windows

FINISHED BLOCK: 7″ × 7″

FINISHED QUILT: 21½″ × 77½″

Two basic pieced blocks make up this quilt. The textured solid fabrics give this quilt a contemporary look.

MATERIALS

1¼ yards total assorted brights for pieced blocks

1¼ yards light for pieced blocks

2⅜ yards for backing and binding

25″ × 81″ batting

CUTTING

Cut from assorted brights:

- 16 squares 5½″ × 5½″ for pieced blocks

- 34 rectangles 1½″ × 2½″ for pieced blocks

- 34 rectangles 2½″ × 5½″ for pieced blocks

Cut from light:

- 17 squares 1½″ × 1½″ for pieced blocks

- 66 rectangles 1½″ × 5½″ for pieced blocks

- 66 rectangles 1½″ × 7½″ for pieced blocks

Quilted by Diane Minkley of Patched Works, Inc.

PIECING

Piece Block A as shown. Press. Make 17 blocks.

Step 1

Step 2

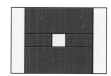

Step 3

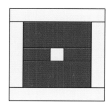

Step 4—Make 17.

Block B

Piece Block B as shown. Press. Make 16 blocks.

Step 1

Step 2—Make 16.

PUTTING IT ALL TOGETHER

1. Referring to the diagram (page 41), arrange and sew the blocks in 3 rows of 11 blocks each. Press.

2. Sew the rows together to form the quilt top.

FINISHING

1. Layer the quilt top with batting and backing. Baste or pin.

2. Quilt as desired and bind.

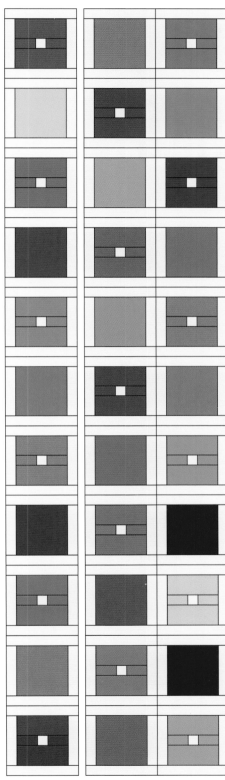

Putting it all together

Quilted by Diane Minkley of Patched Works, Inc.

Quilted by Diane Minkley of Patched Works, Inc.

Chunky Monkey

FINISHED APPLIQUÉ BLOCK: 6″ × 6″

FINISHED QUILT: 18½″ × 85½″

An assortment of striped fabrics are pieced for the base of this simple quilt. Appliqué circles give it a contemporary look.

MATERIALS

1½ yards total assorted stripes for pieced backgrounds

⅜ yard total assorted solids for appliquéd circles

¾ yard paper-backed fusible web

2½ yards for backing and binding

22″ × 89″ batting

CUTTING

Cut from assorted stripes:

■ 16 squares 6½″ × 6½″ for pieced background and appliqué backgrounds

■ 7 rectangles 6½″ × 3½″ for pieced background

■ 2 rectangles 6½″ × 9½″ for pieced background

■ 6 rectangles 6½″ × 12½″ for pieced background

■ 2 rectangles 8½″ × 18½″ for pieced background

APPLIQUÉ

Refer to Appliqué (page 6). Appliqué pattern piece is on page 44.

1. Cut 11 of pattern piece 1.

2. Appliqué the circles to 11 background squares 6½″ × 6½″.

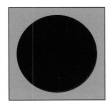

Appliqué circles—Make 11.

PUTTING IT ALL TOGETHER

1. Referring to the diagram at right, arrange and sew the rectangles and squares into 3 rows. Press.

2. Sew the rows together to form the center of the quilt. Press.

3. Sew the 2 end rectangles to the quilt top. Press.

FINISHING

1. Layer the quilt top with batting and backing. Baste or pin.

2. Quilt as desired and bind.

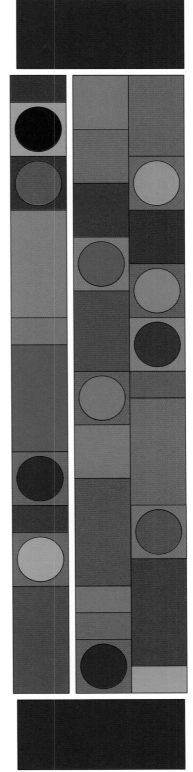

Putting it all together

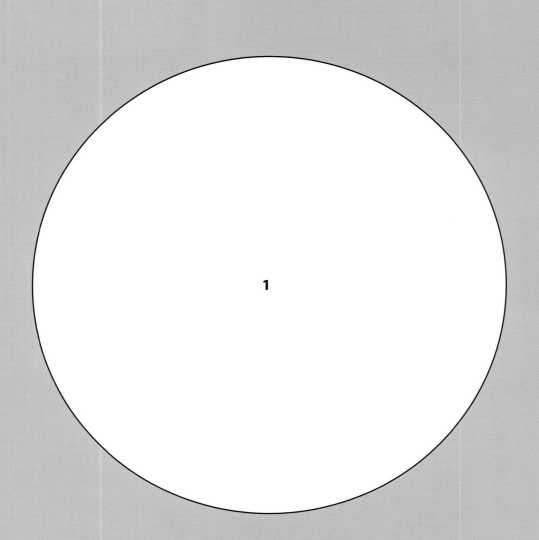

1

Framed Nine-Patch

FINISHED BLOCK: 13″ × 13″

FINISHED QUILT: 13½″ × 78½″

Simple framed blocks made from 3″ squares make up this super-easy quilt. This is a great project for beginning quilters.

MATERIALS

¾ yard total assorted light prints for pieced blocks

¾ yard total assorted medium and dark prints for pieced block borders

2⅜ yards for backing and binding

17″ × 82″ batting

CUTTING

Cut from assorted light prints:

- 54 squares 3½″ × 3½″ for pieced blocks

Cut from assorted medium prints:

- 12 rectangles 2½″ × 9½″ for pieced block borders
- 12 rectangles 2½″ × 13½″ for pieced block borders

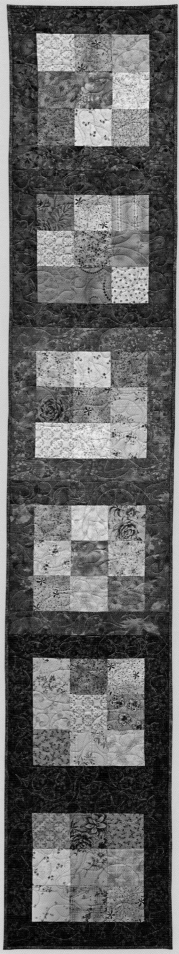

Quilted by Diane Minkley of Patched Works, Inc.

PIECING

Piece the blocks as shown. Press. Make 6 blocks.

Piece blocks.

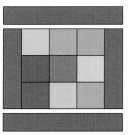

Sew block borders to pieced blocks.

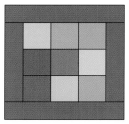

Make 6.

PUTTING IT ALL TOGETHER

Arrange and sew the blocks in a row of 6 blocks to form the quilt top. Press.

FINISHING

1. Layer the quilt top with batting and backing. Baste or pin.

2. Quilt as desired and bind.

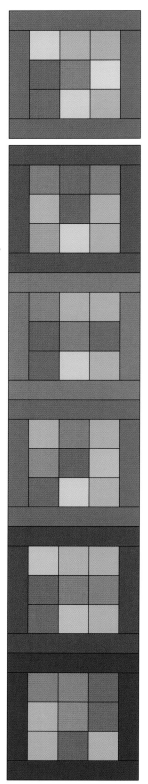

Putting it all together

About the Author

Kim Schaefer is from southeastern Wisconsin, where she lives with her husband, Gary; her sons, Max and Gator; and her dog, Rio. Kim and Gary also have two married daughters, Cody and Ali, and two collegiate sons, Ben and Sam. Kim has two stepdaughters, Danielle and Tina, and two stepsons, Gary Jr. and Dax.

Kim began sewing at an early age, which she says was a nightmare for her mom, who continually and patiently untangled bobbin messes. Kim was formally educated at the University of Wisconsin in Milwaukee, where she studied fine arts and majored in fiber. At 23, she took her first quilting class and was immediately hooked.

In 1996, Little Quilt Company, Kim's pattern design company, made its debut at Quilt Market in Minneapolis. In addition to designing quilt patterns, Kim designs fabric for Andover/Makower and works with Leo Licensing, which licenses her designs for nonfabric products.

Also by Kim Schaefer:

About the Author

Great Titles *from* C&T PUBLISHING

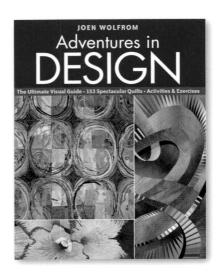

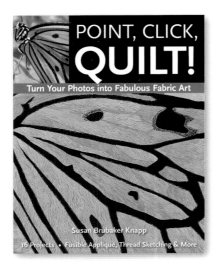

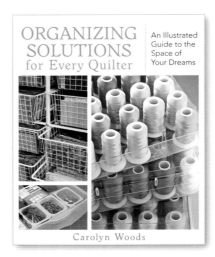

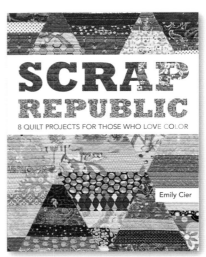

Available at your local retailer or **www.ctpub.com** *or* **800-284-1114**